MAKE MONEY SELLING NOTHING!

THE BEGINNER'S GUIDE TO SELLING DOWNLOADABLE PRODUCTS

Why Information Products?

If you have been pulling your hair out looking for a way to make money online, the search is over! One of the easiest ways to make money is by writing and selling information products in electronic book form. This is the ultimate product for online sales, simply because the potential is enormous!

An electronic book, as you may already know, is not a traditional book that you can turn the corner of one page down to mark your place. (Yes, I am guilty of that!) It is a regular computer file, no different from the hundreds of other files you may have on your hard drive except that it is structured to look and read like a traditional book. You can either read an electronic book on the monitor of your computer, or print it out so that it is portable.

An electronic book can be viewed on any type or brand of computer. You can send them as email attachments or download them from the

Web. Electronic books are extremely versatile! They take up very little room on a hard drive. Some people have hundreds of eBooks on their computer – a library that they personally chose.

Digital Self-Publishing

Digitally self-publishing an eBook is quite different from publishing a traditional book. With a traditional book, you have to pay the costs of any printing yourself if you choose to self-publish. Then, if the book does well and you need to reprint, you have to pay those costs again, which eats into your profits. If you have the goal of having your book published the customary way by a big-name publishing house, get ready for a long wait.

First, your book has to be approved. That can take a year or more, if it happens at all! Most people who have the dream of publishing their book have a folder full of rejection letters to show for their efforts. If by chance your book is approved, it is not published right away. There's a wait for that, too. All told, it could be several years before your book hits the market, and even more time before you see any profit from your labor!

There are no printing costs, and very little waiting time involved with publishing an eBook. Statistics show that eBooks sell better than audio books and paperback books, and information eBooks sell best of all.

What Makes Information Ebooks Such A Special Product?

- Information is extremely profitable.

- There is an unlimited quantity of information in the world today.

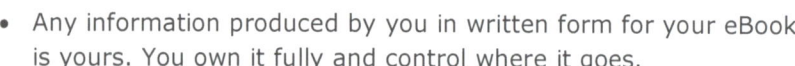

- Information is easy and inexpensive – close to free at times - to deliver to your customers online.

- Any information produced by you in written form for your eBook is yours. You own it fully and control where it goes.

- Information that is new to people, or presented to them in a new manner will have very little competition.

- Your item is different from anyone else's because you wrote it! (It goes without saying here that you can't copy someone else's work and try to pass it off as your own!)

- Information lends itself quite well to cross-selling, a type of sales technique where you would offer a more profitable product at the same time you are pitching your main information product.

- Cross-selling can make even more money for you. Selling a product that goes well with the theme of the information product can double or even triple your profits sometimes. Say you wrote an eBook on dog training. If you offered training collars, leads, clickers, and other items used in your book on the same web site, your customers would be quite tempted to buy them. Consider cross-selling as a way of offering accessories to your eBook. Often, an eBook is given away free with the purchase of an item in order to entice the customer to buy the higher priced products.

- Information also can be used in up-selling. This would be when you had two versions of your eBook – a regular version that sells for one price, and a "deluxe" version with more information that sells for a higher price.

There is really only one product in the world that can meet all of these criteria that are listed above, and that's an information product.

What Are Information Products?

"But what exactly are information products?" you may be asking. "Where do I get all this information from? I'm glad you asked that question! Information products are one of my favorite things, simply because there are such a variety of subjects to write about! An infinite number, really! Let me explain to you just what an information product is.

Information products are fact and data based reports that are one of the hottest things on the Internet today. Take a look at the eBook listings on EBay, if you want proof of this. Do a search for terms like "eBook" or "how to", or even "information Product" and you will see that there seems to be an eBook for every subject imaginable!

Why Are They So Popular?

Why is the online buying public so gung-ho over eBooks? Because information sells! In fact, it could be said that information is one of the best selling products of all time!

How can that be, you might wonder. Not everyone in the world is on the Internet, and there are an awful lot of products for sale floating around both on and offline. Why do people buy information?

Simply because information:

- Helps people in many ways

- Educates people about things that interest them

- Solves problems that people run into in their everyday lives

- Entertains people

- Makes them think

The Perfect Product...

When it comes to writing an eBook, your imagination is about the only limit you will have. Think of all the different subjects you could cover! The possibilities are truly amazing! All things said, in my mind, an informational eBook is THE perfect product. Why have I come to that conclusion?

- The information in that book is your information. It came straight out of your brain. You, and only you, are the master of this information! You, and only you, can decide on what price you want to ask for your eBook.

- When selling information products, you are never going to find yourself low on stock. Write it once, and sell it for years has been my motto ever since I started writing and selling informational eBooks!

- These eBooks are easy to create (okay – I hear you groaning! Never fear – I am going to explain a technique to you later in this book that will enable you to crank out your own information products in less time than you could imagine!

- Some information never goes out of date. Depending on the subject you choose for your eBook, you could sell that same finished product for years!

- The price of a finished information product is NOT based on how much it cost you in time and equipment to produce it! The price you choose to ask for your work is based upon how much value the eBook can deliver to your customers.

- There are ways for you to deliver information products to your customers automatically, without having to be in front of your computer to do it by hand. That means you can be asleep and sell eBooks at 3AM, sell eBooks while you are watching television – even sell eBooks while you are on vacation! You will be able to make sales 365 days a year, 24/7, with the right informational eBook.

The Domino Effect

I've always found that writing an eBook has a domino effect. Once you have written one, you always seem to be able to come up with another subject that you think would make an information product that people would be interested in buying.

Take that book on dog training I mentioned above. After writing that, suppose you decided to write additional eBooks that would outline how to train specific breeds of dogs?

The training method is no different really, but by using the same training information, then adding the breed's history and some breed specific information to it, all of a sudden you have a new information product!

And with more than 800 different dog breeds recognized by the various kennel clubs around the world, suppose you wrote an information eBook for each of those breeds? See what I mean? The domino effect in action!

Think about it this way. One of the main reasons people have and want an internet connection in their homes is because of the vast amount of information available to them on the internet. People of today are information hungry!

Finding Your Niche Audience Over and Over Again

In order to write information products that sell – eBooks that people will flock to your web site to buy, you are going to have to go by the wisdom – or wit – of popular radio and television comedian Red Skelton. "Give the people what they want, and they will come." This sage sentence has been changed by many an eBook writer to go something like this – "If you write it, they won't necessarily come and buy it."

Truer words were never spoken! You may think you have got to do a little research and decide on a niche, or target audience. The audience is the group of people who you will be addressing in your eBook. But you somewhat limit yourself by writing only to a target audience. Many eBook writers would question this theory and think it was a rather radical thing to say, but I think that you need to provide information products that do not fit into one single category.

Let's suppose you decided that your target audience was going to be quilters. You write a smashing eBook about your own easy quilting method and include several original patterns you designed. You place this information product on a web site you created for the express purpose of selling it, and your sales go pretty well; for a while, anyway. Then, it seems like all of your sales potential has dried up and blown away.

Why did you all of a sudden stop selling your eBook at a fairly brisk rate? You're down to just a few sales a month now!

Your sales have slowed to a crawl for one simple reason. You exhausted the market for quilting. Not everyone is a quilter, or even knows a quilter to buy your eBook as a gift for. Someone who is interested in Texas Hold 'Em Poker, or how to arrange flowers, or how to give a great baby shower, is not going to buy your eBook about quilting!

Or suppose you are just passionate about healthy eating. Everyone has to eat, you reason. And so, you write an eBook extolling the virtues of fruits, vegetables, and whole grains, design a web page for it, and sit back and wait for the orders to start rolling in.

You sell 15 or 20 copies before the orders start to slow down, and then grind to a halt. Yes, everyone has to eat, but some people are not going to give up their junk food diets, no matter how persuasive your eBook may be.

So much of the advice available for would-be eBook writers urges them to write about what they love, or what they know best. Sometimes, eBooks like this will do quite well. And sometimes, their authors are very disappointed in their sales.

Why Do Ebooks Fail?

The reasons that most people fail at being a successful online eBook distributors are threefold.

- They write their eBooks about topics that are much too general in scope.

- They pay attention to what someone else says is a hot topic instead of going with their own instincts.

- They go by what most of the online gurus are telling them, and write about "what they love/what they know." You saw the results of that theory above.

So, how do you write eBooks that everyone will be interested in at some time or another? Your eBook has to have something different from the general "how to" eBooks that are being sold all over the Internet. You may well be writing about the same topics, but you are going to have a bit of "Bait" in your book that is going to make your potential customers jump like a fish jumps for a baited hook. What topics are there that every person on earth will have a need for at some point in their life?

Writing For a Desperate Audience

There's not a soul on this earth who hasn't had some sort of problem to overcome. Problems, big and small, are in our lives on a daily basis, whether we want them there or not. Yet somehow, we are able to overcome most, if not all of them. We learn from our mistakes and move on.

Sometimes, the solutions to the problems I have faced have been pretty simple. But, it took me quite a while to figure out just exactly what the solution was, and how I would implement it.

It's that way for most people. They are desperate to solve life's little and big problems, and yet it seems to take forever to figure out the steps needed to do so. That's where you are going to step into the picture.

These people will be the best eBook audience you could ever hope to have. They have problems, and they want solutions... now!

What sort of problems that are common among people would be suitable for an eBook?

1. People who are having financial difficulties, such as facing bankruptcy, poor credit, bad credit, foreclosure. These people are pretty desperate. They would be extremely willing to pay for information that could help them.

2. People who have rowdy pets who need training. Dogs who bark all night long or won't come when called. Cats that refuse to use the litter box, or scratch up the furniture. That sort of thing will have people combing the internet for a solution that you can supply.

3. People who are looking for a way to lose weight. This is always going to be a hot topic, because it's always going to be a problem that people want to solve. There are a lot of different diets, and a lot of reasons why people are willing to do almost anything to take off the pounds. You can mix and match the diets and ideas and come up with a real winner of an eBook.

4. People who want to save money. EBooks about saving on your energy bill, spending less at the grocery store, finding the best online shopping discounts, living frugally how to budget– all of these are issues that some people must face often, and each would make a compelling eBook that would help many people out of a tight situation.

5. People who want to get started selling on Amazon.com, Amazon's new Kindle store has made a lot of people rich in both the Fiction and Non-Fiction markets. Any vital tips and tricks to help them reach that goal can make big bucks for YOU.

6. People who are having legal issues. It may be someone who is trying to collect child support. Perhaps it is someone who is facing a court trial and is desperately seeking information about what to expect. Or maybe it is someone who was arrested for no reason and wants to represent himself in court. The law is vast and varied, and there are many topics that you could write about that could save someone a lot of time and trouble.

7. People who are looking for information on how to improve their luck in the stock market. New investors are especially eager for all the information they can get.

8. People who are having trouble with their love life. You'd be amazed at how many people get online searching for ways to revive a lost love, start a new relationship, keep their present relationship from crumbling, or improve a so-so relationship. They would snatch up an eBook written with them in mind.

9. People who want to quit smoking, clear up their acne, tame their frizzy hair, or solve other personal problems. There are a ton of these that would make great eBooks that people would be thrilled to buy.

This is but a tiny sampling of all the topics that are what people want to know about. Also consider that different age groups want to know about different things. Teen boys are looking for help with video games. Teen girls want beauty hints and relationship helps.

Young working people would pay dearly for eBooks on how to conquer stress on the job, move up the corporate ladder, or even how to go into business for themselves. Young parents would eagerly purchase books on how to care for their colicky newborn. Baby boomers worried about retirement would welcome eBooks on preparation for that time in their lives.

There is definitely a need for this information! When you write about topics that people just have an interest in, they may or may not be motivated to buy an eBook that tells them about it. But, when you have written something that details a way to help them solve a problem that has been keeping them up all night with worry, you can bet that most people are going to be very interested indeed! Interested enough to buy your eBook!

Come on – haven't you yourself Googled a problem you are in the midst of to see if you could find an answer? I know I certainly have, and so have a lot of other people. But many of them will give up out of frustration or lack of time after looking at a couple of web sites.

These people are the ones you want to reach with your eBook. All the information that they need will be gathered together in one easy-to-read format that they can refer to over and over again, online or offline if they take the time to print it out – which they more than likely will!

I know what you are asking yourself right about now. You're wondering how you are going to be able to get the information to write about problems other than your own. While your own problems can be a good place to start, it wouldn't hurt to do some research to try and pinpoint the types of problems that are most common for people in today's world. One way to get data to use is to –

Become an Information Detective

The Internet is full of information – we both know that. And now, you are going to make use of it to research the subject of your first eBook. The search engines are sitting there waiting to do your bidding. Did you know that different search engines can bring back entirely different results? That's why you need to use more than one of them for some really through research. Besides Google, which I think nearly everyone knows about, you also have these search engines to help you in your task ahead:

- Ask.com

- Live Search

- Yahoo Search

- Dogpile

The search engines are where you will go for the detailed information you need to write your eBook. But there is also another source of information that is a fairly untapped source for aspiring eBook authors, and some of these sources are not always found on a regular search using one of the above search engines.

These are the blogs, newsgroups, email lists, online forums and newsletters. There is a virtual goldmine of information related to your chosen subject just sitting here waiting to be tapped. You can find these sources by using a certain set of terms on your choice of search engines. Just take the word that represents the subject you have chosen, and match it with the source. For example, if you are looking for information on insurance, simply type in –

- Insurance email lists

- Insurance newsgroups

- Insurance forums

- Insurance newsletters

You can get a handle of what would be the most popular topic for your first eBook just by taking a little time to read some of these message boards, email lists, and all the rest. These are real people talking about their problems on these forums and such. You never know when you might run across a posting that would spark an idea for an eBook, so it's a good idea to jot down notes as you are reading.

Now, what do you do if for some reason you can't find the information you are seeking by using the search engines? Then you have probably chosen a topic that would not sell very well. If people are not discussing it, they are not apt to buy an eBook about it! Try with another subject until you get a match. Once you do, it's time to write!

The Best Information Source on the Planet - Public Domain

Writing the content for your eBook is not all that difficult – Really! It will make your writing go a lot faster if you are familiar with the subject. You won't need to do much, if any research in order to get the thoughts out of your head and onto the screen. But even if you are going to be writing your first eBook about a subject that you don't have a whole lot of personal experience with, rest assure you can write about it, and write well, too. Right now, this may sound difficult, but with the right research techniques, you can craft a wonderful eBook.

Remember back during your school days when you had an assignment to write a report about a subject you didn't know too much about? What did you do in order to equip yourself with the needed knowledge?

You probably went to the library and read up on the subject, or consulted the set of encyclopedias you had at home, in order to learn all about Saturn or the Civil War or whatever subject your teacher assigned to you. And, you wrote your report based on the knowledge you had gleaned from books.

While I wouldn't advise choosing to write an eBook about a topic that you were totally unfamiliar with, you can write very well about almost any issue with the help of your best friend the search engine. There is information on the web on any subject imaginable that would amaze you.

What Do You Want To Achieve?

- One of the first things you must do is decide just exactly what you want to accomplish with your eBook. Yes – I know you are hoping to make money with it! But, what is your motivation for this book? What do you want it to do besides boost your bank account? Think about how you would answer the questions below.

- Does the information in your eBook serve a real need or impulse that people have? An eBook on how to train your dog to stop barking, or how to painlessly lose 20 pounds would be two examples here.

- When someone has finished reading your eBook, what kind of new understanding, knowledge, or set of skills, problem-solving or otherwise, do you want for them to have gained?

- Is the information you have given in your eBook useful to people? Better still, is it unique? Does it offer the reader something that other eBooks on this same subject more than likely do not?

- Will those who read your eBook know what to do to accomplish the goal it addresses? Will they understand how to avoid bankruptcy, train their dog, or whatever your chosen topic is all about?

If you can answer these questions, your eBook is well underway already, even if you have yet to type the first line of text.

Target The Book To The Audience

You should think about how to target your writing style toward your audience. An easy way to do this is to imagine who you are talking to – and talk to them! Are you writing about video game codes? Your audience will be teenage boys. Is your eBook about how to soothe a colicky newborn? Then you'll be talking to mothers or perhaps even fathers. Explain your subject matter, and write in a simple, conversational tone, but do not talk down to your audience. Picture your audience in your head as you are typing, and you'll find it makes "speaking" to them a lot easier.

As I said earlier, it's always easier to write about something you know, but even then, you need resources to flesh out your book. I suggested that you make use of the wonderful internet search engines to do research to enable you to write an information product eBook.

But, suppose you have come up with a great idea for a problem solving eBook, yet you are having a hard time compiling the data. Or, suppose you just don't have the time to do the research? There is a perfect solution for you! Simply turn to the massive selection of public domain works that are online.

What Is The Public Domain?

You're probably wondering what I'm talking about. The public domain is a humongous range of many different types of materials or "creative works" that are all lumped together and given the title of "intellectual property." Anything that is intellectual property is not owned or controlled by any person.

Also, these materials are no longer under copyright, for it has expired. Copyright expires -

- Whenever a book was published for the first time before January 1, 1923.

- If a book was published at least 95 years before January 1 of the present year.

- If person or persons who wrote the material died at least 70 years before January 1 of the present year.

- No perpetual copyright has been placed on the material.

- No copyright extension has been granted on the material.

It's estimated that about 15 percent of all the books ever written are now in the public domain and no longer under copyright, and this figure includes 10 percent of all the books that are still in print. What this all means is that ANYONE can use these materials.

Any material that is or was from the United States government and several other governmental bodies in this world is excluded from copyright law. It is considered as public domain property as well.

You're probably thinking, 'Well, that's all very nice and very interesting, but what does it have to do with me and the eBook I want to write?

These public domain materials are treasures to anyone who wants to create an information product! Not only are will you find written materials available for your use in the public domain, but also images, audios, and videos!

Okay, I hear you. You're wondering how in the world could anything that old be something that the people of today would care anything about reading… right? Here's a little trivia for you that may make you think. I'm sure you've heard of the Disney movies Snow White and The Little Mermaid, especially if you have kids. Did you know that these movies were once written works languishing in the public domain? A wise Hollywood producer found them there, put a bit of a modern twist on them, and turned them into movies that were a hit with old and young alike – and made a lot of money for the Disney Company! If a big conglomerate like Disney can use public domain material, you can certainly capitalize on it as well.

Here is a tiny sample of some of the public domain information that is available online for you to adapt into a superb information product!

- Mind reading
- Accounting
- Treating High Blood Pressure
- Copywriting
- Herbal Remedies
- Learn to Draw
- Staying Healthy at 50+
- Occult Studies
- Marketing
- Food
- Walking for Exercise
- Stock Trading
- Games
- Wrestling

- Home and Garden

- Movies

- Interior Decoration

- Needlework

- Sports

- Astrology

- Fashion

- Hobbies

- Pets

- Travel

- Disabilities

- Nutrition and Diet

- Sexuality

As you can see, the vastness of this information is absolutely mind-boggling. It's hard to believe that all of this information is free for the taking and is most definitely NOT considered plagiarism, but it is gloriously true.

Don't you think you could find a topic for an eBook just from the listing of rather broad subjects above? All of them break down into further categories, by the way. What a rich resource of information, and it is all waiting for you to turn it into eBooks, articles, reports, how-to manuals, or any other type of information product you can dream up.

I think that perhaps one of the best things about using public domain works to create information products is that not too many people are even aware that this material exists.

They have no clue that there are millions upon millions of pages of well-written, interesting knowledge and gathered facts that they can freely use in any way they want without having to ask anyone's permission.

Anyone can reproduce public domain works, distribute and sell them, and adapt and modify them. Sounds too good to be true, doesn't it?

How To Use The Public Domain

The only caveat to using public domain material is that you must check to make sure that the material you want to use is definitely in the public domain.

You need to insure that you are using the original public domain work as later versions of this work may possibly have been revised or annotated, and that adaptation could have been protected by copyright.

To explain this in an easier to understand manner, think of the original public domain work with a fresh layer of material added to it, and not just the same material written in a different way. The fresh layer is what has the copyright – NOT the public domain material.

So, to be on the safe side, it is wise to have and keep a printed copy of whatever original public domain work that you use for your information material so that if you are ever questioned about your eBook source material (which is highly doubtful) you have proof that you used the original works.

There are four main categories of public domain material that you can choose from to create your information product.

1. Plain, everyday "generic" information such as blank forms, titles, facts, ideas, numbers, etc.

2. Any written material that is still under copyright that has been donated or allowed to be used by permission of the author. Sometimes, out of the goodness of their heart, or for reasons unknown, authors will allow their work to be used regardless of whether or not it has a copyright.

3. Anything written or produced by the Federal government or anyone writing information and/or materials FOR the Federal government.

4. Any material that previously had a copyright, but lost it for one reason or another and is now in the public domain.

I well remember how excited I was when I first found out about public domain material. It was as if my fairy godmother had waved her magic wand and spilled open a treasure chest in front of me! I spent several hours that first evening in mute fascination, just looking through the lists and lists of books on every subject imaginable, articles, pamphlets, and other information that I could hardly believe I could actually use to develop into an information product.

Then, when I discovered that there were several online libraries containing more public domain material than I could ever read in a lifetime, I was hooked. I knew I was onto something really big, and the very next day I was galvanized into action.

I selected a public domain work and developed it into a short but information packed eBook in just one day. I chose this particular information because it blended beautifully with another information product I already had on my web site for sale.

I used it as an upsell (remember our definition of this term above?) to this information product that had been selling for me on a fairly steady basis. I offered this upsell for $9.99, in addition to the $39.99 for the eBook already on the site, and sat back to see what would happen.

In a couple of days, I was shocked and very, very pleased! Sales of my eBook had not only picked up dramatically, but 45 % of the people who bought it also bought the upsell eBook for an additional $9.99! I actually got emails thanking me for the information in the upsell eBook!

I then did another experiment. I chose another public domain book and gave it out for free as a bonus along with another information product I was selling. That free bonus was irresistible, I guess, and since the only way people believed they could get it was to buy my eBook, sales for this one soared as well. To say I was thrilled is an understatement indeed!

But, enough about me and my success with using public domain material. We're here to help YOU use this material to craft an information product that will make a ton of money for you! In a shorter time than you ever dreamed possible, you will have an information product of your own all written and ready to sell. Are you ready? Let's get started!

Creating Your Content With Public Domain Material

Fasten your seat belts – this is going to be a wild ride! No, not really! But the speed in which you will have a finished information product on the screen in front of you ready to market to the public is going to make you think that a rocket sled had something to do with it!

Remember how we learned earlier in this book that people who are desperate for information to solve a problem that they may be having will end up being some of your best customers, just as long as your information product can give them the answers they are seeking and help them out of what they perceive as dire straits?

Remember how we talked about the need to discover a niche market – over and over? You'll find that each individual problem that you create an information product for can be its OWN niche. Often, you can spin off some of these problems and write a second and even a third eBook about the same general subject.

When you do this, you are almost assured of good sales, because the people you helped solve problems for trust you and your writing now. They believe in you, and anything else you write on the subject that interests them will be seen as a "good thing", and they will probably want to purchase other eBooks you write on the subject.

Here's a good example. A couple of years ago, I wrote an information product in eBook form on how to housebreak a puppy or a seemingly un-trainable adult dog in 2 weeks, guaranteed. It sold like wildfire. I suppose there must be a lot of people out there who are having trouble housebreaking their dog! About 6 months after the release of my housebreaking eBook, I pulled some material from the public domain (a U.S. government publication) about traveling with your dog. I changed the wording around a bit, and added some writing of my own. By the way, this is known as a **derivative work** as the finished product was derived from the original public domain material.

By the time I was done with this eBook, it had turned out to be a nice little doggie travel guide complete with descriptions and the toll free reservation numbers of pet-friendly hotels and motels across the United States. I pitched it to the dog lovers on my mailing list, most of whom had purchased my previous eBook (more on mailing lists later in the book – they are a fantastic marketing tool!) and gave them a link that sent them to the sales page (we'll get to that later as well) for the eBook. Roughly 45 percent of my mailing list purchased this little book for $19.95, and it was all made up of free information they could have found for themselves, but chose not to for one reason or another.

I think you would agree that vacations and housebreaking are far from being in the same niche! Yet, both subjects addressed a need in the lives of these pet owners. My purpose for veering a little off subject here is to point out to you that had I not ventured out of my dog training niche, I would not be having the continued sales of my dog travel guide. Don't limit yourself! With each subject you choose to write an information product about, try to think out of the box. Be creative, and watch your profits grow!

Okay – back to work now. You are going to choose a subject for your information product. You'll notice that in my dog vacation book, I made use of the research methods mentioned in this book as well as using public domain material. I used Google to track down the addresses and telephone numbers of hotels and motels who accepted pets. I read traveler's reviews of these accommodations, and then summarized what I had read in my own words to create my listings. Public domain materials and Google – or any search engine for that matter – work well together.

Where To Find The Public Domain Information

There are several online resources where you can find the free public domain books, brochures, and literature you will use to create your eBook. Here is a list of a few of the better ones –

- **Project Gutenberg**
  www.gutenberg.org A great place to start, as all of the materials here have been checked rigorously for any copyright.

- **Ibiblio**
  www.ibiblio.org is "the public's library and digital archive". There are many good choices for information products here.

- **Manybooks**
  www.manybooks.net There are more than 20,000 eBooks here available absolutely free. Check out the nice collection of "how

to" books here. A how-to eBook is nearly always a very good seller!

Most, if not all of the books at Ibiblio.org and Manybooks.net are in the public domain. But I cannot stress enough to you the need to make absolutely certain that any work you choose to use is not protected by any copyright at all. A new law was passed in 1998 that's called the Sonny Bono Copyright Term Extension Act, or the CTEA for short.

This law was the brainchild of the late California congressman Sonny Bono, the same Sonny Bono who was partnered with Cher as the singing duo Sonny and Cher in the 60s and 70s. Sonny was killed in a skiing accident slowly before the bill went into effect, so he never got to see the fruits of his congressional labors come to pass. Basically, the law added 20 years to most items that have a copyright. There will not be any new works joining those already in the public domain until the year 2019. So, be very careful and check out any public domain material that you are going to be working with.

Choosing Your Subject

Choose your subject with care. Remember that there are lots of information product eBooks floating around cyberspace, but they vary quite a bit in quality. Yours will stand out because of the quality of the material that will be included, and the new, unique perspective you will give to the subject.

Some subjects are never in danger of being outdated. Others are decidedly stale! How can you know that the subject you are thinking of writing about will be a fresh, interesting read for your customers? One way to do this is to take a systematic approach.

You're going to start off by making a list. You can either do this on your computer, or by using a pen and paper. I'm one of those people who can think better if I am doing things the old-fashioned way, so I tend to use a notebook that I call my "idea book" to jot down thoughts as they come to me.

- Make a list of all of the different things that you are interested in and know something about.

- Make a list of the things you are interested again, but do not know very much about.

With your list in hand (or on the computer screen!) do some research to find out –

- Whether or not people have been looking for information on the subject recently.

- Whether or not people that have been searching for this information would be willing to pay for it, and able to pay the price you think your finished information product would be worth. More on pricing your product later in this book.

- Whether or not the demand for this information has already been met by how many eBooks containing this subject are already on the market. Remember, too that there is a chance that the demand for this information has already been exceeded. It would be pointless to write another eBook on the same subject if this were the case.

Ideally, the topic you are thinking of writing about will meet all three of the above criteria. If it doesn't, you'll need to pick another topic that does.

How can you tell whether or not people have been looking for information on a certain subject? Thankfully, this is pretty easy to do. There are several online sources that you can take advantage of that will help you to determine if your topic idea has merit.

[Wordtracker](#) is a free keyword suggestion tool that is very useful. Simply type in a word that relates to your tentative topic. Let's say you decided to write an eBook about how to avoid a divorce. If you type the keyword "divorce" into Wordtracker, you'll get back up to 100 keywords related to the original word AND an estimate of the daily volume of searches of these keywords. There is also an adult filter on Wordtracker that you can choose to use, or not. For example, here's the top ten of what came back for me. Note that this information changes on a daily basis!

Searches	Keyword
293	shaq divorce
2134	Divorce
996	hulk hogan divorce
669	john denver divorce
519	marie osmond divorce
466	garth brooks divorce
447	lionel Ritchie divorce
412	divorce public records

387   divorce records

384   state divorce laws

What can we determine from these very interesting and rather surprising results? As you can see, celebrity divorces are HOT. An eBook that had information about the divorces of celebrities that are popular at the time you are writing your eBook would sell quite well. You would simply do your research and collect this info from the web, compile it, and put it in eBook form. You would not need public domain material to do this.

There also seems to be interest in state divorce laws. An information product that had a listing of the divorce laws for each of the 50 states, certain countries of the world, or both, would be very popular. This is where public domain material would come in quite handy, as there are government publications in the public domain that have this information already compiled for you.

Then, there have been quite a few searches on just the word "divorce" – 387 in a 24 hour period. This is proof enough that your original topic idea – how to avoid a divorce – would more than likely be a subject that people would be interested in purchasing an eBook about.

The URL to the Wordtracker web site is -
http://freekeywords.wordtracker.com/

Another source that you can use to check out the freshness of a topic idea is the Yahoo Buzz index at http://buzz.yahoo.com/ . Yahoo Buzz is a collection of the most popular stories from all over the internet, chosen by people who could well be your information product customers. Top stories can be about:

- entertainment

- sports

- world news

- business

- health

- lifestyle

- politics

- travel

- science and technology

Yahoo Buzz covers almost every subject that people has an interest in, and is a great place not only to check out how pertinent your topic is, but also to kick start an idea for you to develop into an information product.

Honing In On Your Subject

One of the most important rules of eBook writing is focusing solely on the subject at hand. If you had purchased an information product about how to avoid a divorce, you would not expect to see a recipe for children's play dough to pop up in the text, now would you? Of course not! The people who will be buying your eBook do not want to waste their time on information that is irrelevant to the topic. They paid their money to read about one thing! They are looking for solutions to their problem or an answer to the question that's been bugging them – and they want these solutions and answers as fast as possible!

You Absolutely Must Be Specific With Your Subject

The more specific the subject is, the easier it is going to be for you to sit down and write about the topics that people are desperate to know more about. A precise topic is also going to lead more people to you when the time comes for you to market your eBook. Your intended audience will find you on the internet by doing a search for a keyword or a keyword phrase which, to them, is relevant to the topic. If someone was searching for information on candle making, for example, they would go to a search engine and type in -

"How to make candles" which is a very specific search term that will bring back the kind of results they are looking for.

If that person typed in the search term "crafts" they might eventually find some instructions on how to make candles, but these instructions would be mixed in with a whole lot of other instructions for soap making, beading, decoupage, tole painting, and a host of others! They chose a search term that is much too broad, and would probably stop their search in disgust after a page or two of results if they had not found what they were looking for.

It's a heady feeling to take an idea that was born in your head and create an information product out of it without the kinds of restrictions and rules that you would have to abide by if you were writing a book for submission to a publishing company. Writing your own products gives you a sense of freedom and creativity like no other I know of.

Quality Is Key

I often feel as someone who has produced many information products as if I better understand how the people who created some of my favorite music must react the first time they hear one of their songs on the radio. The sight of my very first information product, complete with illustrations and a bright, colorful cover almost brought me to tears! To see the results of my work as a finished product, and to know that my words were going to help someone else made me want to get started on another project right away!

But as eBook writers, you and I have a responsibility to our customers. They are going to be paying out their hard earned money in the hopes of getting some answers, so you want them to feel satisfied with what they received for their money.

This means that we have to create a high quality product, or all our work will have been for nothing. Whenever I develop an information product, I want the people who purchase it to feel as if they got some information that they couldn't have obtained anywhere else – information that is different from what they have seen before, and that may well have the potential to alter their lives for the better.

When you make use of public domain material, the chances are quite good that the information your customers will be eagerly reading IS information that they have been unable to find anywhere else. I'm sure you have heard of the term "wisdom of the ages".

Some of these older public domain books and articles contain timeless information that is still perfectly fresh and useful in today's world. Often, the older the information, the better, as changing times and ways of accomplishing things have managed to allow some of the old fashioned, tried and true ways of life and lore to fall by the wayside.

So, it's sufficient to say that you want your eBook to be thoroughly researched and a valuable resource for anyone who reads it. You might not think it is necessary to research public domain material. Some information product authors do, and some don't. I am one of the ones that does research anything I pull from the depths of public domain, and here's why.

The Power Of Research

I want to make sure that the author of the public domain material I am using had ideas that go along with the general thinking of the public today, or that are not so far off base that instead of being thought of as helpful tips, they are thought of as an oddity, or something nostalgic, as in "from the olden days".\

It's got to seem fresh, even if it is old. There are ways you can put a modern spin on some information, which will "freshen it up" quite a bit, but other information needs to be carefully considered.

Here is an example for you to think about. Suppose I decided to do an information product on household tips. I'm moving right along, compiling the home economics information I am finding in the various government publications from the 30s, 40s, and 50s. It's an enjoyable task as the subject interests me, and I am actually learning some things as I work. I run across a paragraph about the care of furniture.

Now, you know that furniture back in those days was pretty much all made of solid wood. Mahogany, rosewood, oak... good, REAL woods, not like our particle board and laminate creations of today! So when I read the sentence about oiling furniture, I pause to reflect on it.

Oiling furniture is something I have never heard of, nor was it taught to me during my growing up years when I was being shown how to keep house. So, I decide to Google this topic to see what comes up, and learned that wood and oil play well together. In fact, real wood will soak up oil like a houseplant soaks up water! People rubbed oil on their furniture to keep it from drying out and cracking, and to preserve its luster and useful life.

This apparently works well, or we would not have the antique furniture present in the world today. But if you were to try to apply oil to say, an entertainment center purchased from a mass merchandiser that is NOT made of wood, you would simply end up with an oily mess to clean up!

If you were to include this tip in your eBook, your customers would read it and probably think, "Huh?" unless they were owners of antique furnishings and thus acquainted with this chore. This tip would not be considered fresh or timely in the least. However, the very next tip I ran across in the public domain material seemed to be something that I could adapt for the furniture of today.

"To remove the water mark rings from wooden tabletops and other furniture that have been left behind by iced tea and other cold drink glasses, take two tablespoons of your best mayonnaise (this was in the days when people MADE their own mayo!) and spread over the water ring, covering it completely.

Place a linen napkin (no paper napkins or towels back them!) over the mayonnaise to make sure the area stays moist. After 6 hours, but preferably overnight, wipe the mayonnaise away. The water mark ring will have vanished, as the mayonnaise has been absorbed into the ring, taking away the white color and restoring the natural hue of the wood."

Since some of today's furniture does have an authentic wood TOP while the rest of its construction is made up of pressed or particle board, this household tip would still be pertinent for those women and men keeping house today, and would be good for inclusion in an eBook of household tips.

These tips, however, are not ones that can be modernized in any way, and would not be useful unless you were writing an eBook titled "Strange Household Tips from Grandma's Kitchen" or something similar.

"To remove tobacco smoke and odors from a room, fill a pail into which you have placed a couple of handfuls of hay with water. Place the pail in the center of the odiferous room."

"Dip a towel into a mixture of half white vinegar and half hot water. Wring out towel and vigorously swing it around your head several times until tobacco smoke and odors have left the room in question. "

I don't know about you, but I don't see any way to change either of these "tips" for use in today's households! Neither of these tips would be a valuable resource for the homemakers of today. That's why you must think about the information you are including in an eBook. You must read it through someone else's eyes instead of your own. You would be surprised at how many times this little exercise will help you to see parts of your eBook that might better be deleted.

All About Your Sales Letter

One of the main things that your sales letter needs to do is persuade your audience that the information you have compiled is well worth the money they are going to pay you for it. Why is this necessary? Because, like it or not, you are going to have competition, and you are going to have to show your audience that your writing is what they are looking for.

Competition is unavoidable, and that's all there is to it. You know that as well as I do, and if you don't, type in a common and popular keyword like "cooking". See how many cooking and/or recipe sites there are online? Now type in the search terms "cooking eBooks" and see what comes back.

Amazing, isn't it? To someone who didn't know too much about how the information product market and the internet works, looking at a list like that would discourage them from ever even attempting to create and market an eBook. So much cooking and recipe information is free right from the web, so why would someone pay for it... right?

Wrong. Cookbooks are among the top selling information products out there. Those people involved in the creation and marketing of cookbooks are all in competition with each other, yet they manage to get along quite peaceably.

I've dabbled in a little bit of cookbook authoring myself, and the last time I checked, there was actually a Yahoo group for those who write cooking and recipe eBooks! They discuss tips on marketing, formatting, editing writing a sales letter that reaches out and grabs the customer, and other tips for success.

Why do they get along so well together? Think of all the different TYPES of recipes there are! Even though all of these people are authoring recipe eBooks and are in competition with each other, it is an amiable competition even though the information used to write these eBooks is much the same.

You may find that the same thing is happening with one or more of your eBooks, especially if you choose not to use public domain materials and are working instead from you own idea with some search engine research thrown in for good measure.

Even though your writing is sparkling and witty, even though your information is fresh and timely, and even though you are making a few sales, things are not going as swimmingly as you had thought.

When this happened to me around the time my first information product went on the market, I went so far as to purchase several eBooks with the same subject as mine.

 I was "checking out the competition" so to speak. These eBooks weren't cheap (it was around this time I discovered that I had also vastly UNDERPRICED my first information product – more on pricing later in the book!) but I was desperate to figure out what I was doing wrong.

Do as I say, don't do as I do! I was so eager to see my competitor's eBooks that I neglected to pay very much attention at all to the sales letter pages that went with them. I just clicked the "Buy Now" button in my haste and either downloaded the eBook then and there, or waited for it to be delivered to me in my email. Lo and behold, when I sat down to peruse my purchases, I was more than surprised.

You'll notice that I did not say what subject my first information product was about, and there's a reason for that. I do not want to call attention to the authors of these works, who are still producing and selling information products on the same subject from time to time. If I mentioned the subject, it might make it too easy for people to figure out just which authors I am talking about.

I clicked through several pages of text in amazement. I am not bragging here, but the eBook I had written was far better, both in content and in style. I couldn't figure out why I was having such slow sales when my competitor's sales seemed to me to be pretty brisk. Thinking maybe I would see the reason if I went back to the web pages where I had purchased the eBooks, I did just that, and this time, I paid attention to the sales letter page that went with each eBook.

That was when it all clicked in my brain, and everything suddenly made sense. The reason that my eBook was not selling briskly, and the eBooks of my competitors were doing quite well was the SALES LETTER PAGE and nothing else. Compared to my own sales letter page, the ones belonging to my competitors were works of art.

They **seemed** to prove beyond a shadow of a doubt that the information in the eBooks they represented was the Bible and the Holy Grail of information concerning that particular subject, all rolled into one! I wondered if I were the only customer who was disappointed with the quality of the eBooks that I had purchased.

If you based your decision to buy on the wording in the sales letter, as most people do (and I didn't) then you would be in for a rude shock when you began to read the eBook. These eBooks my competitors had written had sales letters to go along with them that performed their jobs perfectly and as intended– they made sales for their authors – but did not represent the information product properly!

This is very important, for, as I mentioned above, the essence of a sales letter is proving to the customer that the information in the eBook for sale is well worth what they are paying for it! In fact, it can be said that the sales letter is the key to being successful in the information products business.

Why Sales Letters Work (And Why They Don't)

I'm going to stop right here and give you a few facts about the information products business that you might as well know now.

As the quote goes (some say Abraham Lincoln said this while others give credit to poet John Lydgate) "You can please some of the people all of the time and all of the people some of the time, but you can't please all of the people all of the time."

Some customers will think your sales letter IS too long, and say that there is far too much buildup. They may even say the letter is too much of a hard sell. If you shorten the sales letter, then other customers will say that it's too short and doesn't give them enough facts to aid them in making a decision to buy the eBook. If you try to take the middle road and go for a medium length sales letter, some people are still going to complain about the length.

You're also going to find yourself the recipient of some rather irate and some whiny emails from people who are going to be doing either one of three things –

- Complaining about the price you are charging for your information product.

OR

- Asking you if you could make an exception "just this once" and GIVE them a copy of your eBook.

OR

- Challenging your information because no one would actually be giving away "good" information for free (This would be when you are giving away an eBook as an incentive for the purchase of another information product.)

You aren't going to be able to get away from people like this. They're a part of the human race, and therefore here on earth to stay. You can choose to answer these emails and politely point out that no one is holding a gun to their heads and forcing them to buy, explain that if you made an exception "just once" that you'd feel as if you should do it again and again, or asking for sources to prove that your information is "bad".

To reiterate, your sales letter should please YOU. It should have the information in it that you think is necessary to get across to your prospective customer just why he or she should purchase your information product. Keep in mind also that you can use this same sales letter for the life of the information product it was written for.

Find An Angle

You need to think about the point of view that the person who is reading your sales letter is in at the time they read it. 9 out of 10 people will have one thought in the back of their mind when they are reading – "What's in it for me?" It seems horrid to think of people being this greedy, but it's the truth.

They are taking the time out of their busy lives to read your sales letter because they are looking for a solution to a problem that they have, and they think that maybe your eBook has the solution. Instead of hinting at the contents of your eBook, tell people what the information in the eBook can do for them.

One way to get this across might be to let your sales letter tell about how the information in your eBook helped YOU to overcome a problem in your life, and what you hope that other people will be able to do with this information as well. Customers who are seeking answers will respond to this, as it gives the sales letter a more "human" touch.

Another way could be to hand out a free copy to several people on your mailing list and ask for a testimonial in return. Tell them that you would like to use your testimonial to promote the eBook. This is often done in the eBook world. I have taken several colleagues up on an offer like this, and in return got even more

publicity for my own information products because beneath my testimonial is a link to my web site where people can go to see and purchase my products.

One thing is for sure about sales letters, and it is a truth that won't change anytime soon. There is no perfect sales letter, and there is no imperfect sales letter. The only kind of sales letters in existence are effective and non-effective ones.

Now, let's go and learn how to create an effective sales letter!

Start your sales letter off by letting the customer know that you have been through whatever problem it is they are having. Whether it's trying to achieve a lasting weight loss, manage pain, stop smoking, get rid of bad breath, beat stress in the workplace, or some other problem – **empathize** with your reading audience!

Talk to them as if they were sitting with you at dinner and you are involved in a one-on-one conversation with them. Tell them about your own experiences with

- Trying, and failing to lose twenty pounds before that class reunion.

- Battling a bout of arthritis pain during your last vacation that left you unable to enjoy your trip.

- Quitting smoking for a week and then picking the habit right up again.

- The pain and embarrassment of having your kids tell you that your breath smells just like the dog's breath does – in the middle of the grocery store - LOUDLY.

- How you get so stressed out at work that you sometimes slip into the bathroom for a quick cry to relieve the tension.

Research, Don't Make It Up!

Here's an important point. If you are writing about a problem that you have **NOT** experienced, you are going to have to do more research . Public domain information is voluminous and usually quite through, but it lacks that human touch, that human emotion that is going to jump out of your sales letter and into the minds and hearts of your readers. You are going to have to find someone who has gone through the same thing themselves so that you can better understand the problem, and why it is so crucial that a solution come to light for it.

Needless to say, do **NOT** attempt to make up problems you have had in order to save writing time. They won't ring true. People who actually have the problem will definitely be able to tell the difference if you say something like,

"I wanted a cigarette so bad I didn't know what to do. I decided I would smoke one, even though I felt guilty right before I lit up."

Instead Of

"All I could think about was a smoke. My hands shook as I thought about opening a fresh pack, taking out a cigarette, and putting it in my mouth, and lighting it. I couldn't stand it any longer. I went to where I had hidden a pack of cigarettes earlier in the week, got them out and ripped them open hurriedly. I had one in my mouth in record time. But right before I lit it, a wave of guilt washed over me, and I knew I shouldn't smoke it. Nicotine addiction won out though, and smoke it I did."

Which one of those paragraphs sounds like someone who knows more about what it's like to try to quit smoking? If you guessed the second one, then congratulations. It was kind of obvious though, wasn't it? That sort of raw emotion is what you are going to have to capture for any problem that you write about in order to let the reader know that you understand what they are going through in trying to control their problem. Even if your story is painful for you to tell, or embarrasses you totally, tell about it. Use as many details as you can to convey the feelings of despair that these problems can cause you to feel.

But - where can you find people who are going through various sorts of problems if you are going to write about a problem you have never had yourself?

There are several places on the internet where you can find online forums where people talk about anything and everything. It's perfectly okay to lurk in these forums, and read the postings. You can glean vast amounts of information this way that can help you not only with your sales letter, but with your eBook, too.

How can you find out what subjects are being discussed in these forums?

- Boardreader.com is a veritable oasis of themed information. It searches quickly and concisely for any term you place into the search box, and also suggests ways that you can refine your results. The results that come back also include the name of and a link to the actual forum where the discussion is taking place. You can really get a feel for almost any problem there is when you read some of the passionate discussions that take place on these forums! Other links where you can check out forum postings include -

- Forumzilla.com is similar to Boardreader in that you type the word for what you are looking for in the search box. Forumzilla does not seem to come back with as many results as Boardreader, but is useful in case you need to attempt to read some alternate boards other than the ones covered by Boardreader.

If the problem you have decided to write about is one that you have had yourself, you may decide to participate in one of the forums and discuss it with others. This way, you can ask questions which will be useful in assisting you with your sales page. The more believable your sales letter is, the more sales you will get from the people who read it.

You probably have already done this when doing the research for your eBook, or maybe you concentrated on web sites with information about the problem you are writing about rather than sales letters of those who are selling information products about the same subject you are. In other words – your competition.

Research The Competition

Read these sales letters carefully. What are they promising that their information will do? Do they sound as if they are familiar with the problem? Are they charging for the information, or are they giving it away as a gift for buying some other information product that they are selling? Can you learn anything from these sales letters about what you should and should not put into your own letter?

Back to your sales letter now. Information is information, you know. There is only one way to quit smoking, for example. You just stop – but there are several methods commonly used to help smokers to stop. There are several ways to stop stress in the workplace, and also several ways to conquer bad breath. How is your information product different from the rest of those on the market? What kind of twist have you given to the information to make it unique?

Do you have new information that your customers may not have ever seen before? Make sure you stress that your information is fresh, well researched, and accurate as well. In your sales letter, tell your potential customers why your information is different, and what that difference can do for them. Tell them what this information has done for YOU. Stress how your life has changed because you applied the information that you are offering in your eBook to your own problem. Talk above how wonderful it is to live without that problem, and to know that you have the key to solve it should it ever rear its ugly head again!

Mention how hard you looked for a solution to your problem on the internet. Tell how you spent hours on end attempting to find something, anything that would help. Tell about how you ordered other eBooks you found online that were supposed to help with the problem, only to find that the information in them was either outdated, or did not work. Stress that nothing you tried helped your problem UNTIL you discovered the information that is included in your eBook.

Never Give Away Your Information For Free!

You can talk about the information, but of course you do not reveal what it is in the sales letter! You instead can talk "around" your problem's solution, give hints, etc but never reveal the actual "meat" of your eBook.

Perhaps the most important point of all for a sales letter is this one.

Tell your potential customers that the information in your eBook can help them with their problem NOW. This is vital to the success of your information product! People who have problems that are eating away at them don't want to wait any longer than they have to in order to get their problems resolved. If you can include a sentence or two in your sales letter that will give your potential customers hope, then the battle of getting them to buy your product is half over!

- You want your potential customers to know that you understand their problem.

- You want to come across not necessarily as an expert (thought that doesn't hurt) but as a person who is sincere and believable in what they have said concerning the problem.

- You want to stress to your readers that YOUR product is the one that can help them control and/or get rid of their problem.

You can do all three of these things by choosing the words that will start out your sales letter with care. These words are probably the first thing your potential customers will see, and must be attention grabbers in order to interest readers enough for them to continue reading and not click away from your page to go and do something else.

You want to choose a clear concise sentence or two for your headline, and the sentences or sentences MUST grip your potential customers firmly and interest them to continue reading!

Sentences like –

"Have you tried to kick the nicotine demon out of your life numerous times, yet failed and gone back to smoking? With the method outlined here, you can be an ex-smoker much sooner than you ever dreamed possible!"

Work much better than this sentence would, true though it is –

"Stop Smoking Now the Easy Way!"

Next, tell your story. Tell how this problem was devastating for you, how it was making your life miserable and that there were times when you weren't sure if you would make it because having the problem had begun to control your life. You'll find that people will identify with you when you begin your sales letter this way.

More about your sales letter, the key to your success, in the next chapter!

More About Writing The Sales Letter

We're continuing our rundown of how to best write a sales letter that will make your eBook sell in this chapter. We ended the last chapter by describing how the problem you are writing about was ruining your life will make your potential customers feel a bond with you. When they believe that you understand what they have been going through, an invisible link forms between you and them. It's a pretty strong link, too. People with problems of one kind or another are often, and sadly, lonely.

Create A Feeling Of Kinship With The Reader

Never would I suggest that you capitalize on someone's loneliness,

and truthfully, that isn't what you are doing here. But it's a proven fact that lonely people often seek out others to share their loneliness with. When they decide that you understand their problems, often they feel as if you are their friend, too.

This never hurts! In fact, I still email back and forth with several wonderful people who I met because they wrote to thank me for the information I made public in an eBook I wrote a couple of years ago. A feeling of kinship is always helpful in gaining someone's trust, and the trust of your audience is what you are trying to gain.

Expand on the fact that you tried other eBooks to solve your problem. Tell about how you had such high hopes each time you purchased a different one, only to have those hopes dashed when the information did not do the trick for you. This will tell your potential customer two things.

- You know how it feels to buy an information product and then not have it work for you. They will reason that since this happened to you, you would not want to inflict that same feeling on anyone who might purchase the eBook you are selling.

- Since you tried other avenues on the internet in the form of purchasing other people's information products to try and solve your problem, searching web sites for information and none of these avenues worked for you, your potential customers will also reason that you would not be promoting an eBook that did not solve the problem.

Disclose Some Weakness

This may sound very counter-productive, but in order to make your information product even more believable, you need to discover and make known some weakness in your program. Here's an example –

If your eBook is about trying to quit smoking, saying something like –

> "Although this method of quitting smoking has been almost like a miracle for me, I will admit that I have still needed some willpower at times to get past the psychological withdrawals of not smoking."

Your open admission that your information is not 100% perfect tells your readers that you are being very honest with them, and also helps to temper their expectations that the product is going to help them with no effort on their part. This is important, for you will always have a small segment of people who will complain if a product does not work to suit them.

By admitting that the person using the problem-solving method may also have to use some willpower, you are saving yourself in the event that these people complain that your information did not help them. Then, you can counter their accusations by asking them how they used the information. It won't take long to determine those who honestly try to follow the program as opposed to those who only go at it half-heartedly.

Justify The Price

Another thing you should cover in your sales letter is the reason why your eBook is worth the price you are asking. You should tell your readers that the information you compiled is actually worth much more than the price you are asking, because it is different and better than the information in the other eBooks currently out on the market.

Ask your audience how much is it worth to them to be rid of the problem that is currently bothering them, and then point out that being free from a problem is absolutely priceless – that no monetary value can actually be placed on something so wonderful as the freedom one feels when a pressing problem has left their life. This helps to reinforce the value of whatever price you end up deciding is best for your information problem.

The Matter Of Refunds

This also brings up the question of offering a refund to those people who are not satisfied with the price, or satisfied with the product after they purchase it. Should you do this, or not? I always offer the option of a refund. Sometimes, this can actually help you to make a sale, as people feel as if they have nothing to lose if they have a money back guarantee on the product. I have had people actually act very surprised the few times I was asked to issue a refund, and did so promptly.

They mentioned that they had purchased other information products with a supposed money back guarantee, yet they never saw their money when they requested it. To me, this sounded rather as if these people made a practice of buying eBooks and then returning them for a refund, as they seemed to be very familiar with the ins and outs of getting a refund! But, aside from that, issuing refunds promptly when you are asked to can only be good for your business image.

Ask For The Sale

When you get to this point in your sales letter, it's time to ask your potential customer to buy your information product. Stress that your ordering process is secure and that they have nothing to fear by using their credit card online, or that they can also pay you via PayPal, even if they do not actually have a PayPal account. Of course, you will have set yourself up to accept credit cards and PayPal payments, which will more than likely only take a couple of weeks to apply and complete the process from start to finish.

The Power Of The p.s.

Most savvy information product entertainers end their sales letter with a postscript, or a P.S. as it is commonly called. After saying everything that we have mentioned above in a sales letter, you may be wondering what in the world you could have to say in a postscript? This is your last chance to point out any last words of wisdom or encouragement concerning your problem-solving techniques that you have outlined in your eBook. You can also use the last of the sales letter to warn readers of the possibility of the price of your product increasing sometime in the future, and it might be wise for them to take advantage of the current price right now.

It's also common those who sell information products to place something in this section about themselves to give their customers some reassurance as to who they are dealing with when they purchase your eBook. You can tell something about your personal life (other than what you have already mentioned when telling about how you solved your problem) or mention other websites that you may own. Give links to these so that they can visit them and find out more about you and your products.

Your postscript has almost as much of an impact on potential customers as does the headline. Whereas the headline is the first thing your audience will see, the postscript is the last... and sometimes the first! People have been known to read sales letters from the bottom up, so make sure that your postscript is a powerful one.

Testimonials

Did you get several testimonials from people who read your eBook before you put it up on the web for sale to the public? If not, now is the time to do so. You need to make sure that these testimonials are very believable, so that when your potential customers read them, they will see that other people were able to rid themselves of their problems by using the information you are making available. Testimonials are also good to have on your sales page so that anyone who may be a little skeptical about whether or not your eBook will help them can see that it has actually helped people.

Benefits And Consequences

You can have the best information product on the entire web, but if your sales page is not a real winner, you will not be able to sell nearly as many eBooks as you would with a sales page that is tailored to help people see that you have a solution to their problem. You want to show yourself as THE person who can solve their problems for them. You want to stress to your audience what will happen in their favor when they purchase your information product, and also stress what the consequences will be if they do not take this opportunity to solve the problem that has been a thorn in their side for so long.

Other Things Not To Forget

The sales page must show your audience why your product is unique from any of the others that are being sold on the web. It needs to point out to them the weaknesses of these other products, and then emphasize why your product is better able to solve the problem they are having. A good sales letter also points out to your audience that the benefits of purchasing your information product far outweigh the cost they will pay to purchase it.

Sales letters need to emphasize these things, which are what potential buyers look for most of all:

- Less expensive

- Best value for their money

- Works better than other solutions

- Most up to date solution on the market

Consumers are a perverse lot. They always have been, and they always will be. Why else would they demand an information product that is the cheapest, yet more to date, more functional, and a better value than other eBooks being sold? These things don't seem to go together at all, yet are what anyone who produces information products should strive for.

Pricing Your Product

Pricing your eBook can be a puzzle if you have never done it before. You and you alone will have to decide how much you should charge for your work. It is quite important that you take some time to think about this, and don't just pull a price out of the air indiscriminately. You have to realize that figuring out the right price is crucial to whether or not your information product will be successful. Don't think that the best solution is to charge a small amount, so that more people will be able to buy your eBook.

Remember, people who buy things are contrary. Though they want to buy products at low prices, they sometimes grow suspicious if a product costs too little! They have the mistaken idea that since you are charging a small price, the product must not be of very good quality. Little do they realize that most people who charge small amounts for eBooks are newbies who do not know any better, and set their price on the low side to try and benefit the greater good.

But, these newbies soon realize that in order to succeed in making a profit with an eBook which they are selling at a low price, they would have to sell thousands of them! Newbies often have the opposite problem, too. They price their product on the high side, see that they are not making many sales, and lower their prices. This can cause a host of problems as time goes on. How? Let's say you start selling your eBook for the sum of $49.99. Then, you see where your competition is selling an eBook at a cheaper price, so you lower your price in order to be more in line with them. You figure they know more than you about pricing since they have been "in the business" longer. But instead, the people who purchased your eBook at the original price you set get wind of the fact that you lowered your prices, and get a bit miffed about it.

Deciding on the best price for your eBook is part of marketing it, which we will discuss in more detail in the next chapter.

Marketing Your Information Product

If you really want your information product to be a success and bring the profits in for you, you are going to have to investigate how to market a product like an eBook online, and once you are familiar with the steps you must take to do so, you'll need to put them to use.

The Sales Letter

The first step in marketing is the item we discussed in detail in the previous chapter called the sales letter. I can't emphasize just how important the sales letter is going to be to your selling success, but suffice to say that if your sales letter is not a good one, you are not going to sell very many eBooks.

The Web Site

In order to market your information product, you need a web site. There are many options for this, most outside the scope of this eBook. If you are reading this, you probably already have a web site of your own. If you don't, you can just use your favorite search engine and find out all you need to know about creating one. Don't put this off, because you definitely have to have a web site in order to be in the information product business!

Advertise Your Site

Let's just assume that you already have your web site all in place and ready to go. Now we are going to discuss a few ways that you can bring people to your site There are many, many things you can do to market your information product, and having a web site with your sales letter displayed on it and a download link where people can download your eBook directly to their own hard drive (after paying you for it, of course!) is possibly the best one. But no matter how well laid out, colorful or fancy your web site is, if people aren't coming to it, you aren't going to sell a thing. You have to **promote** your web site so that people know about it.

Url Submission

You can start out by submitting the URL of your webpage to the main search engines on the net. It's quite easy to do. Just visit the main search engines such as

- Google

- Yahoo

- AOL Search

- Ask.com

- MSN

and look for the link on each that says "Add your URL". Just follow the directions, and presto! Your web page is now listed in the search engines, and when people type in a search term that has to do with the subject of your eBook, your site will pop up in the results.

SEO

However, your web site will do much better in the web site rankings if you optimize it for the search engines. This is called SEO or Search Engine Optimization. The way this is done is to make more than one webpage on your site – generally around three pages are sufficient. Each page should be focused on a specific keyword or key phrase. What this means is that you will have these words on the page several times… but not too many times or the search engines won't like your page as much.

Many people don't realize that there is something called a "search engine spider" that crawls all over the web visiting pages and adding their information to the search engine's ever growing list of web sites and their contents. So, the addition of the keyword pages to your information products website will insure that you get listed in the search engines.

Links

Links that point to your web site from other sites will help to bring even more people to view your sales page and web site. And, the major search engines see this as a good thing. The number of links that you have coming into your web site makes these search engines rank your pages higher, which means your site will be closer to the top of the first page of results that comes back when you do a search. This is a very good thing, because it is natural for people to click on the links on the first page, and not necessarily even look at the links on the second and subsequent pages.

Directories

There are directories that you can submit your web site to as well. One of these is called the **Open Directory Project,** and it provides information to all of the major search engines. A perk that comes with listing your web site here is that Google especially is rather impressed with a link from this web site, and will rank you higher because of it. But, you will have to be patient when listing your site here.

It can take a long time for your information to be included, as real humans are the ones who are overseeing the input of this info, and there is a waiting list. The same thing is true for another directory you should list your web site with, **Yahoo! Directory**.

There are instructions that you should follow carefully when you are submitting to this directory, and try not to be too wordy in your description, or the Yahoo editors will have to do some tweaking to make it fit.

Promotional Articles

Another way for you to boost the visibility of your web site is to write articles that have to do with the subject of your information product and submit them to one of the many article websites. A good one for you to try is ezinearticles.com . A link to your site is included in a box at the bottom of the page the article appears on, so this is a good way to rack up more page views.

Web site and mailing list owners come to these article repositories and can choose articles for free to use on their own web site or in email newsletters, so there is the possibility that your article will be chosen by someone for this purpose, providing you with even more page views that will hopefully turn into sales.

In order for this to happen, though, your article needs to of course be well written, but also have the proper keyword density. By this, I mean that your chosen keyword needs to be used in the article several times in order for it to be picked up and listed with search engines such as Google.

Google Adwords

A great way to advertise your web site is to use Google Adwords, a very popular way for people to attract attention to their online business or product. You have probably seen these Adwords as you surf around the web. They are the "Sponsored Links" that you see at the top and along the right side of a search results page on Google's main site, and also on partner sites.

People will see your ad when they have used a search term that is one of the keywords or keyphrases that you have bid on to use in your advertising. **You do pay** a small fee every time someone clicks on one of your ads. This can cost you a few dollars a day, depending on the number of clicks, but if you can get 4 or 5 sales per day from the added traffic, then it is money well spent.

You can choose how much you want to spend each day in fees at the time you are setting up your Adwords account. Generally, the more money you can afford to spend each day, the more your ads will be shown. The more your ads are shown, the more possible click throughs you will probably receive. Since click throughs are what can turn into sales, this can be a win-win situation for you!

A neat little Adwords trick that has worked quite well for me is to be very precise about the keywords and key phrases that I choose to bid on, because I am going to use these keywords in the actual Adwords advertisement. This way, the keywords are right there in front of the web surfers to catch their attention, and my click through rate has been a lot higher ever since I implemented this trick.

You do need to keep a close eye on your Adwords situation. You don't want to keep paying for click throughs if you are not getting any sales from them!

It is easy to go in and change your keywords, so it might be a good idea for you to have a back up list of words ready and waiting, just in case some of the ones you have working for you stop producing any clicks.

Google also has a tool that will turn out to be quite useful for you, as it will tell you which ones of your keywords someone clicked on and ended up making a purchase on your web site. It's called a conversion tool, and it is one of the neatest things I have ever had the pleasure of using! It is really good to be able to tell which keywords are producing sales for me. It helps you to know when you need to change out a keyword, or leave things just like they are.

But you might now have the funds to use Google Adwords just yet, even on a small scale. Don't fret – as long as you have time to spend on it, you can do many things to very effectively promote your web site for free or for a very reasonable cost.

A Word About Backlinks

You should think about how you want to go about getting backlinks to point to your web site. What is a backlink, and why should you want to have them? Well, most people in the eBook business have a theory about backlinks. They know that the general idea is that people will link to a page if they think the content of it is good.

And as far as the search engines are concerned, the more backlinks, the better. The most valuable kind of backlink is from a web site that has the same theme or subject as the eBook on the web site you are attempting to get backlinks for. You should set aside a block of time once or twice a week to spend some time building these backlinks.

One super way to get backlinks is to post in the blogs of other people, and especially the blogs that belong to college and university students. These blogs will all end in .edu, and are full of posters who may well provide backlinks to your site as well as increased traffic.

You must choose with care which blogs to add your interesting, thoughtful posts to, as you would not want to post a paragraph about your weight loss eBook in a cooking blog! There's a formula you can use with the search engine Google to ferret out the blogs that will be relevant to your information product. Just type the following into the Google search box -

site: .edu inurl:blog "post a comment" –"comments closed" –you must be logged in" "weight loss"

This will bring back a listing of .edu blogs where you can post a comment without having to register or be logged in. You can change the words "weight loss" to whatever your information product's topic is about. Post some good, quality comments and don't spam these blogs.

If you think your posts look like you are fishing for backlinks without having much interest in the blog where you are posting, so will other people. This could get your post deleted, and all your time posting will have been wasted. On the other hand, post like you mean it, and you will get some great backlinks, increased traffic, and more sales. You'll find that having quality backlinks is a very simple method of sending prospective customers to your web site. As a matter of fact, most information product gurus know that the number of backlinks they have is crucial to their success.

Why You Should Have a Mailing List/Newsletter

If you are really serious about selling your information product and creating a nice source of passive income for yourself, you absolutely cannot do without a mailing list and newsletter of your own. Why do you need these tools? They are quite possibly two of the most valuable assets that you can have to help you to achieve your marketing goals for your eBook.

So, if you are serious about this information product business, you definitely need a mailing list and/or a newsletter.

What To Include

Some people go so far as to send a complete chapter from their eBook to their mailing list, sort of as a teaser, to allow them to see what they are missing by not purchasing the entire thing. Others don't believe in revealing their work in such a fashion, even if it means that it gets them more business in the long run. They send out friendly emails which talk about the subject of their information product, then at the end with no pressure ask that the reader consider buying a copy.

Occasionally they will include articles that have to do with their eBook's subject. These could be articles that they have written themselves, or articles that they have found at a free article bank. You must maintain a mailing list for it to be successful!

Much like authoring an eBook, you must give the people who sign up for it some value for their time spent in reading it. You must also adhere to a regular schedule for sending out your newsletter. A haphazard habit of sending out a newsletter whenever you think of it is not going to bring many customers your way.

Persuading People To Sign Up

How do you get people to sign up for your mailing list? You should always place a link to your web site inside of your eBooks, along with a polite urging to join the mailing list. On the web site where you are promoting your information product, offer your visitors a chance to sign up for a mailing list/newsletter. You can mention briefly what the newsletter will discuss, but  there is no real need to go into detail… those who are interested will find out soon enough!

This is a good time for a give-away, as often this is what convinces people to join a list. Another eBook besides the one you are selling is a perfect thing to use as a give-away product to those who commit to joining up. This does not have to be an eBook you write yourself, but can be one of the many free ones you can sign up for that is relevant to your information product's subject.

Sequential Autoresponders

With a web site, you are going to need a sequential autoresponder.  Otherwise, you can expect to spend a lot of time sitting in front of your computer sending out emails once your mailing list gets underway! A sequential autoresponder can make following up with people who expressed some sort of interest in what you have for sale very easy and fast for you.

It makes communication automatic, yet it looks as if you have taken the time to sit down and write a cheery, chatty email just to them! The autoresponder personalizes these emails, greets the person by name, and looks to be personally from you. The people you are contacting through an autoresponder are going to feel as if they have a sort of relationship with you, based on these emails.

Sequential auto-responders are rather new in the online world. They haven't been around for too very long. Predating the sequential variety of autoresponder was the one time autoresponder. It could only send out one email at a time. With a large mailing list like I hope you are going to have, it would be almost counterproductive to use a onetime process.

The sequential autoresponder can be set up to email responses in the order that you choose them. You could perhaps send out one when someone first signs up, another one two days later, another one on the fifth day, then skip three days and send out yet another on the ninth day.

The automation of this autoresponder is its beauty. Once you set it up to work for you, you usually only have to do it once. It will continue to do what you have asked until you stop it. It will send out responses over and over, 24/7 around the clock! Once a person signs up on your web site for your mailing list, they will receive a confirmation email requesting that they click a link to confirm that they want to be subscribed. This is necessary, as it is proof that you are not sending unwanted email, or spam to them. Once they do confirm, the autoresponder sends them a welcome message, and then they will get more email messages based on the way you set it up.

You may think that you can get by with using the "I am on vacation" autoresponder that is standard with your email program. If you had a very small mailing list, this might work, though it is doubtful.

Plus, there's a good chance you could be accused of sending spam and place your internet service in danger of being disconnected. Besides – you are going to have many people on your mailing list! So, you need a service that is capable of handling a large number of subscribers.

There is a fantastic sequential autoresponder services that I would recommend. It is called Aweber.

- Aweber is as fast as greased lightening when it comes to sending your messages and helping to build your list. As a matter of fact, you probably couldn't send and receive as fast as Aweber does for hundreds of thousands of users.

- They are the industry leaders in autoresponders. You needn't be intimidated by using something so powerful, as Aweber as all sorts of help files for you to peruse.

- Aweber has the best record of any autoresponder for making sure your emails make it to their intended destination.

- Aweber is very reasonably priced. It only costs around $15 to $20 per month as of this writing.

Now that you have your autoresponder all set up, what sort of emails are you going to be sending out to your present and potential customers? Have you thought about developing an e-Course that ties in with the subject of your eBook?

Ecourses

What's an eCourse? An electronic teaching series which consists of anywhere from five to seven short lessons of about 600 words each. Your autoresponder will send these lessons out on a schedule that you choose - every day for one week, or every other day for two weeks are the usual choices. What the eCourse will do for you is establish you even more so as an expert in the subject that your information product is about.

They are quite easy to write, and the autoresponder makes distributing the course a breeze. Anytime a person is thought of as an expert, people who are interested in his area of expertise are going to look up to him and want to emulate him to some degree.

The addition of an eCourse to your arsenal of marketing tools will enable you to draw even more potential customers to your web site, and should, along with the other marketing tricks you have learned, boost your sales beyond your wildest dreams.

By this time you have probably started to mull over a few ideas for your own information product. I urge you to research your choices, make good use of public domain material where applicable, and do some intelligent marketing. Before you know it, you will be a bestselling eBook author!

www.ingramcontent.com/pod-product-compliance
Lightning Source LLC
Chambersburg PA
CBHW040320220526
45473CB00009B/2503